Grandfather's Robin

Gillian Bickley

Proverse Hong Kong

2020

Grandfather's Robin collects 63 poems written or completed since Gillian Bickley's last poetry collection, *Perceptions*, was published in 2012. To some extent these new poems reflect her activities, thoughts and experiences during the period from 2012, including in Hong Kong and Andorra. But some concern previous experiences, recorded in earlier years. At least one – the sympathetic and affectionate portrait of her maternal grandfather – is a synthesis of childhood memories. She responds to people, to fellow-creatures (defined from a biblical perspective and including mammals, birds, trees, the moon and human manufactures), considers social behaviour (including as a response to political change, and as reflected in exhibited works and their visitors), and also reflects on concepts of eschatology and survival. She aims to communicate as simply as possible and to elicit or extend what her readers may already know from their own different lives and experiences.

Gillian Bickley was born in the UK and has lived mainly in Hong Kong (but also in Nigeria, West Africa, and Auckland, New Zealand) during her professional career as a University teacher of Literature in English. Five of her poetry collections have been published (*For the Record* (2003), *Moving House* (2005), *Sightings* (2007), *China Suite* (2009) and *Perceptions* (2012), and her collected selected poems, *Over the Years* (2017).) In 2014 at the 18th International Festival, "Curtea de Argeş Poetry Nights", held in Romania, she was awarded the "Grand Prix Orient-Occident Des Arts" by the Festival Board. Bickley is one of the Hong Kong poets discussed in Agnes S. L. Lam's study, *Becoming poets: The Asian English Experience*. From time to time she now teaches creative writing at the School of Professional and Continuing Education, University of Hong Kong. Gillian is also known as a historian who takes special interest in nineteenth century Hong Kong. Her biography of the founder of Hong Kong Government Education, *The Golden Needle: the Biography of Frederick Stewart (1836-1889)*, is regarded as definitive. More recently, her editions, *Through American Eyes: The Journals (18 May 1859 - 1 September 1860) Of George Washington (Farley) Heard (1837-1875)* (2017) and *Journeys with a Mission: Travel Journals of The Right Revd George Smith (1815-1871), first Bishop of Victoria, Hong Kong (1849-1865)* (2018) joined an earlier work, *Hong Kong Invaded! A '97 Nightmare* (University of Hong Kong Press, 2001) (an edition of the 1897 work of future war fiction, *The Back Door*), and have gained attention. With her husband, Verner Bickley, she founded the International Proverse Prize for unpublished book-length fiction, non-fiction, or poetry and the International Proverse Poetry Prize for single poems.

GRANDFATHER'S ROBIN

Gillian Bickley

Proverse Hong Kong

Grandfather's Robin
by Gillian Bickley
First edition published in paperback in Hong Kong
by Proverse Hong Kong
Copyright © Gillian Bickley, August 2020.
ISBN-13: 978-988-8492-07-7

Distribution and other enquiries to:
Proverse Hong Kong, P.O. Box 259, Tung Chung Post Office,
Lantau, NT, Hong Kong SAR, China.
Email: proverse@netvigator.com;
Web: www.proversepublishing.com

Cover image, "stream", watercolor and acrylic on paper,
by Steven Schroeder (stevenschroeder.org), 2020.
Used by permission.

Cover design by Artist Hong Kong.

British Library Cataloguing in Publication Data
A catalogue record is available
from the British Library

PRIOR PUBLICATION ACKNOWLEDGEMENTS

'Hospital Visit', in *Coming to our Senses*, Hong Kong Writers' Circle, 2019.

'Song Of The Potato'. First published in *Antologia Mundial, La papa, seguridad alimentaria*, ed Jackeline Barriga Nava, Bolivia, 2019. (The anthology was part of a UNESCO-supported project to emphasise the importance of the potato for food security.)

Cecilia Claase, workshop on behalf of Hong Kong Women in Publishing Society, 'True Record', 'No Need to Hurry!', 'Constant Parade'.

Various issues of *Imprint*, the annual anthology of the Hong Kong Women in Publishing Society (HKWiPS), as follows:
 'White Gloves', 'Sincerity' (under the title, 'Riddle'), (Vol. 12, 2013); 'Comfort', 'You' (Vol. 14, 2015); 'Familiar', 'Gifts', 'Patchwork' (Vol. 15, 2016); 'Aching for Trees', 'Company' (Vol. 16, 2017) 'Survival', 'Cat Cradles', 'A Single Dahlia' (Grouped under, 'Summer Thoughts', Vol. 17, 2018); 'Song of the Uprooted Trees', 'Visions on Show' (under the title, 'Ten^2 Inches Sculpture Exhibition'), 'Early Morning' (Grouped under, 'Man and the Natural World', Vol. 18, 2018); 'Three Bells in a Pyrenean village' (Vol. 19, 2019).

'Outcasts from Reality (short version)', in *Outloud TOO*, ed. Vaughan Rapatahana, Kate Rogers, Madeleine Slavick, MCCM Creations, 2014.

Dedicated to Verner Bickley
with love

AUTHOR'S INTRODUCTION

Where does a poem come from? – Often, from something seen, felt, heard, thought or experienced. Sometimes, in response to a prompt from outside the writer's own consciousness; an invitation to compete, for example; or a group activity setting a challenge. In due course, a call for submissions may lead to revisiting, re-editing, re-interpreting. And when putting a collection, such as this, together, Wordsworth's words, "emotion recollected in tranquility" ('Preface' to *Lyrical Ballads*, 1802) feel very apt. The words written earlier recreate the experience, thought, sound or feeling, which caused them to be written down. It is a good to make a record such as this.

GRANDFATHER'S ROBIN

Gillian Bickley

PEOPLE
Portraits
Responses to glimpses of other people's lives

12   Grandfather's Robin

PEOPLE

Portraits
Responses to glimpses of other people's lives

GRANDFATHER

My grandfather was a quiet man;
an allotment near the railway line,
where his working life was spent,
gave him additional quiet.

"Ask your grandfather to take you there,"
the family suggested.

He showed me his shed,
but most of all the robin's nest
with blue eggs or bald young,
and an alert bright-eyed brown nesting bird,
on a high shelf in the dark,
which a curious small girl could just
stand tip-toe to see.

"Don't touch it now!" he warned,
quite sternly, for him.
"She'll abandon the nest, fly away,
perhaps never return."

His own mother had done that;
died when he was fourteen.

For the rest of his life, on one day of the year,
the quiet man was quietest of all.
"What's the matter?" his wife or daughter
(my mother and grandmother) would ask.

"This was the day my mother died,"
came his unchangeable reply.

YOU[1]

Your eyes are blue as a cloudless sky,
Your skin softer than a fully-ripe peach,
Your hair golden as the sun,
Your spontaneous smile, sweet as sugar-cane,

Your actions,
kind as parental love
in various of earth's species,

Your thoughts,
deep as the ocean,
surprising and bright as lightning,
lateral as the horizon.

With abundance of Nature's qualities,
your sophisticated soul is hidden,
beneath their surfaces.

August 2015

WHITE GLOVES

As we walked on the wide
Andorràn pavement,
crowded, some fifty yards ahead,
by a watchful group;
gathered outside the city church,
on the corner of a narrow, medieval, street;

for the time being,
ignoring the waiting hearse;

As we passed citizens
reclining on city seats,
conveniently placed
for watching
the passing show,
and passing
the time of day;

"Espagnole? – Spanish?"
an elderly promenading gentleman asks,
inclining graciously at my side.

"No, English!" I say, surprised.
"Oh! I do not speak English," he replied.
Then, speaking the language of his heart, continued,
"*Mi madre* – my mother – wore white gloves like yours."

He raised his white panama,
bowed in a polite and dignified way,

and walked on to the funeral
of his recently passed friend.

Andorra la Vella,
August 2012

SCALLOP-SHELL

Inconspicuous, with swift steps
walking through the city,
he yet had things to say:

On his back-pack, the United Nations flag.

Hanging from his neck, on his chest,
two half scallop-shells making a whole.

"I've done the walk, made the pilgrimage
to Saint James of Compostela;
understand the world's need for quiet unity
and for faith. In my quest is definite assertion."

For those who see and understand,
you reinforce what they suspect
and truly know.

The others continue shopping,
enjoy the sun,
travel in cars
for their material ends and means.

Andorra la Vella,
Summer 2012

COMPANY

An old man with white hair
sits in a garden chair
in a remote [Pyrenean] [mountain] hotel,
singing a song in his own language,
no-one near.

He has taken his small dog for company
on this lonely holiday,
and a small bag to carry him in, here and there;

But his singing shows he needs… he wants
human emotions…human thoughts to share.

Hotel Coma,
Ordino,
Andorra,
Summer, 2015

PATCHWORK

You sit among bright scraps,
placing and patching for hours:
patterns, pictures and people,
Night light and day light,
Bright lights and dim.

You work quickly, pensively,
but do not fully control;

Adding and building
until the work of your hands
says,

"I am finished.
"Stop now.
"And my name is 'orchard' or 'illuminations' or 'this is where you
stop'."[2]

And what other power is making you?
Placing, shaping, trimming for years?
Not fully controlling? (For you have free will.)

Can *you* ever say, "I am finished, complete;
And my name is 'patience', 'service', 'energetic love'"?

Another will say it;
And has said, "This patch … immortal diamond,
Is immortal diamond."[3]

6 September 2015

WELCOME TO COME ALONG!

There I am, standing around in the City Hall – that
big empty space near the snack-bar, box-office and enquiries desk.
and I see – unusual sight! –
a foreign woman, gazing at the splendid billboard,
erected by the Central Government.

"Welcome to come along!"
I shout to her –
Perhaps rather loudly, as I am wearing my new headphones,
listening to western music. –
"Welcome to come along!" I shout to her again.

She looks at me – unsure – but
she nods – slightly unfocused;
not wanting me to reject her, in
case it was not really her I was addressing.

She makes several enquiries, then walks out through the garden,
into the high block lift lobby.

I follow her, watch, as
she enquires here too, follow her
into the lift; and I want her
really to know it was she I had spoken to. I shout,
greeting her as the lift doors
close. She and the two other
passengers move backwards slightly;
and I notice, on her shoes, some sticky paper.

To show my friendliness further,
I point to it, bend down, remove it;
see another piece, remove it too.

Now she knows it is she I addressed.

"That's very kind of you," she says, slightly shy.

The doors open. Taking the two
removed strips of sticky paper,
I propel myself outside,
to the rubbish bin.

"Goodbye lady, it was nice to meet you!"

Hong Kong,
2011
City Hall

COUPLED

I saw *her* first;
holding six roses –
florist-wrapped –
straight up
before her,
as she walked unseeing through
the painted green
pretend central city garden.

Then I saw *him*,
tall, thin,
holding two heavy bags,
one on each side,
their weight hanging them straight.

His careful
trudging
looked caring.

Did she know her life's husband
was still certainly her beau?

Such a pity; I think, no …

Hong Kong,
June 2012

BUS DRIVER

"Take Care!" as I get on,
"Take Care! Good Luck!" as I get off –
So amiable and kind.

Like all of us, he has deadlines to meet;
but he waits, ensures we will not fall,
before he puts his foot down,
drives off.

Not an easy job, I'm sure.
He looks tired, unwashed perhaps,
so early in the morning, today.

He has his own life too. –
A family to care for and support? –
To live with, at least?

I hope they say to him,
as he embarks, each day,
for what is, of course,
a dangerous and taxing occupation,
"Take Care! Good Luck!
"Come home safely!
"Enjoy your day!"

Hong Kong,
April 2012

SOFT

Sometimes, when we speak, our lives unroll
before those we speak to, without our knowing.

"Eat this; it is soft," the young waiter says,
pointing at some egg pudding, or blanc-mange.

And we see behind him a large family
of grandmas and old aunts, toothless,
needing something soft to swallow
without too much chewing.

And we see the kindness he has been taught at home.

Hong Kong,
15 June 2013

GOODBYE

For Ah Oi

Once or twice you were singing in the kitchen.
But when I asked you what the words meant,
you were embarrassed and stopped.

"An old person is a treasure in the house."
You were our treasure
but today you gave back the keys.

You came in a pretty top
and I was dressed in flowers too
to receive you.

You apologised for retiring
but said it was a long way to come
– two hours each way –
and you were sorry that you could find
no friend to replace you.

I gave you a cheque;
We took photos and you
limped out the door.

The end of an era.

Twenty-four years, just like that...

10 October 2016

GEOFFREY BONSALL, RIP[4]

A long life has much to say for it;
one must select what to say. And
life itself – however long – is itself
a selection from what might
have been done. You chose, it seems,
to serve other men's words and meanings –
in libraries, on a publisher's then editor's
desk, as speech-writer and breaker of codes.

And the place you chose to live – somewhat
predetermined by your place of birth –
Wuhan, Hubei, in China (a missionary's son) –
also, as it seems, signposted
the areas for your life-time's work
(Asia and Asian Studies mainly) –
necessarily excluded – or at least
diminished – other foci that you might equally
have beamed your search-light on.

We have benefited from these choices;
also from your courtesy, concern,
your conscientiousness, and yes,
your curiosity and cushioning too.

You persisted in teasing-out
other men's meanings. Doubtless
you knew your own meanings too.
Is there anyone left who will unpick
your puzzle for us all to read
and then know you better than we did?

July 2010

**HOSPITAL VISIT:
KINDNESS, MAINLY WITHOUT WORDS**[5]

I
I wave at her as she's pushed along –
Frail pale old lady in a wheel-chair.
She smiles a little and waves back...
waves back again, passing me, as the swing-doors open...
waves back, half turning her head,
as she passes through to the black gulf outside.
"Goodbye, goodbye!"

II
In the bone-test queue, a lady responds to my request
and helps me tie the borrowed hospital gown.
Her husband, waiting with her, wordlessly suggests
I should wear the second one also, still lying in the basket.
(Well yes, that would be more decent, I realise,
understanding now, split down the middle as they are, why there
are two!)
Later, she suggests I should copy her,
move up, occupy an emptied seat.
"Where we sit will determine the time of our turns," she gestures.
I suspect she misunderstands, but do as she wants.
She is well-meaning and kind,
believing now, what her husband already knew,
that they are certainly, in some respects, more expert than I;
and, like him, quietly accepting a duty of care.

III
The young man, a half-full urine bag at his side,
waits in line for his coffee. "How're you doing?" I ask.
"It hurts to clean it myself", he says.
"If I find I can't do it,
"I'll be here another week...."

Later, as I wonder where to sit,
he leaves the queue, helpfully comes over.
"You can use it," he reassures,
pointing at a table he half occupies with his things.
"I can't sit here; I'm just charging my laptop.
I still have things to do."

IV
In this venue, our shared humanity is all that counts.
Small gestures of interest and kindness are all we have to offer,
as we ask the frightening, necessary, system to investigate or heal
us,
send us forth to fight and live the joys of life another day.

Hong Kong,
2019

CORNEAS GIVEN AND RECEIVED[6]

The *South China Morning Post*, Saturday, 14 April 2018, p. A8, c.2, has a news item, 'Dying woman donates eyes to "look" for lost son.'

Corneas Given

I embrace this chance
to see you once again:
Dying I give my eyes
Indeed to strangers
But the force of my desire,
to see – to <u>see</u> – <u>you</u>, will surely
give them understanding
of my wish, my pain, my longing
to see, see, see again <u>you</u>,
my twice-ten-years vanished son;
and the force of my desire
will give them power – and will –
to convey your image
to my vision, where,
breathless and eyeless now,
I languish, longing; and loving you.

Corneas Received

We <u>will</u> search out your son
Our – your – eyes in us
will scan each crowded street, each country path,
looking for the man
your young son
must now be. We will ask
likely youths to show their feet,
looking for his scarred heel,
which will be, not an Achilles' heel,
but a healing to your immortal soul, when found.
Our gift of vision for *your* gift of sight.

April 2018

WEDDING PHOTO

Unlike Dorian Grey...[7]

The photo fades in the sometimes too-bright sun;
<u>Our</u> colours change too, but love smiles through
the repeated questions and concerns,
answering the only question that matters,
"Yes, I do!"

RESPECT

"The young have no respect these days!"

Small nun:
shaved hair now producing a stubble;
eyebrow pencil;
small felt/cotton shoes;
semi-rimmed eye-glasses.

She knew to avoid, and not
even to glance surprise
at the rough young man
who pushed in front of her
in the designated lane
for queuing at the MTR.

October 2017

FUNERAL OF MRS DOROTHY COLLINS (1914-2002)

So that is that, all over then. And not
a bad send off, when you think of it.
The quiet room. The careful few, anxious to do
aright by you. Your students mainly. – Adult
men in suits, one with a broken arm. –
Not quite sure of the form, but willing to conform
to the quietness, that was your life-long practice.

"Very well!"[8]

Hong Kong
2002

STICKS AND STONES WILL BREAK MY BONES,
BUT WORDS WILL NEVER HARM ME

An acquaintance,
whose sexual proclivities
few doubt,
resigned his cushy job
at a local university,
and now works freelance.
Among other things, he reads the news.

This morning's news
contained an item
about someone
who wished
to pervert the course of justice.

"Pervort – pervert – pervort – Pervert," he stumbled.
I did not know he was
so sensitive
about
the word.

1970s or 1980s

BOLIVIAN VISITORS

Liquid luscious rhythmic
        bird human water
            notes
sing of trees and heights
        the joy of living inhabiting
           sound and green

Bent weather-beaten denim-trousered
half-hobo – their habitué – gives
applause… is recognised,
his now sought approval reconfirmed.

Small, shaven-haired
girl in pink sways in
time. They kindly play the
parents through their child,
as they sing.

The rattle, the rhythm, the liquid
notes chirp, warble, flow, on…

Hong Kong,
25 March 2018

FRIENDS FOR A TIME[9]

The world is surprisingly full of them,
people who notice, who care and dare:
Dare to thrust a bundle of string in the hand of a stranger,
helpless in a post-office;
Dare to pick up the expensive, carelessly left-behind camera,
leap off the mini-bus as it accelerates, sacrifice the fare,
stretch out comfort
to the ridiculously running after it, panicking owner!

Dare to stand and talk to a pretty beggar with baby, listen to her
story;
Dare to approach the foreign woman fallen on her face,
ring her husband, dial "999", report to the ambulance crew;

Seeing smoke, to bang on a neighbour's door;
Open the last fare's wallet to find out his contacts,
ring him, speak in an alien tongue,
drive to his place after a long shift has ended,
and return it, refusing reward.

And I, am I such a friend to strangers, too?
What have I done or do?
Well, I listen to stories.
If you talk to me, I won't walk away,
however much of a hurry I'm in;
I say, "Mmh, yes, indeed!"
And, after we've parted,
I remember what you told me,
remember your story for quite a long time
and yes, I feel for you,
accepting exactly what you say,
your version of reality, as true.

Like the Good Samaritan in the original story,
some dare to interpret what they see and hear,
dare to judge what's required, and then provide it;

Others, <u>un</u>like the wedding-guest in Coleridge's rhyme,
importuned, stop and listen
to stories that burst confine.

None are friends for life,
but certainly friends for a time.

Hong Kong,
January 2017

LOVE
Saint Maximilian Maria Kolbe (1894-1941)[10]

I read your story and wanted to write about you:

Your pre-adolescent dream of Mary,
offering you choice –
a white crown for purity,
or a red crown for martyrdom –
and your decision,
"I accept both".

Your life of many actions,
determined and shaped by her
who had offered only sacrifice.

And the final sacrifice,
which in time made you a saint.
"Take me in place of him. I am a priest.
But he has family and wife."

The witness of the man who lived:
"As long as I have breath...
it is my duty...
I will tell people about his heroic act of love."

What else could there be to say?

JOSEPH SCHERESCHEWSKY (1831-1906)[11]

"Was his method wrong?"
I think he asked,
rhetorically indignant.

"His whole intention was to serve
a distant goal; that, one day,
the Chinese Bible
would be read by thousands.

"And the day is now!"

*

Think of that!
A hundred years and more
after you spent your days
translating, translating, nothing else;
a Chinese priest, here in Hong Kong,
confirms your life, your work.

All scholars (who labour
in truth and honesty)! –
May your work also win,
in time, such sympathetic praise!
The intention, the spirit you display,
is what we love, admire…

23 March 2016

FELLOW CREATURES

FAST FORWARD – HARAMBE I[12]

Yes, it's true,
As a child, I was taken to the zoo,
to see the gorillas. And I saw him,
so strong and calm,
and truly a protective father to his family.
And I loved him.
It was love at first sight.
And I wanted to be with him,
to experience his love and protection.

I expressed my desire many times to my family.
But no-one listened or cared.

So I rolled under the barrier –
it was quite easy, and I did it quickly –
And I fell down into his moat.

Oh bliss! He came to me. He picked me up.
He held me on his arm, then stood me up
and wondered at my clothes. And then – oh horror! –
a loud noise hit him. His grip on me loosened.
He and I fell.
And I was taken from him. – For ever! –
My love had destroyed him.

In the years that followed
I thought about this lesson
and avoided love, certainly its expression.

But every day, now no longer a child,
I go to that zoo, visit his family,
and say, Sorry, Sorry Sorry!

1 June 2016

FAST FORWARD – HARAMBE II[13]

Yes, it's true,
As a child, I was taken to the zoo,
to see the gorillas. And I saw him,
so strong and calm,
and truly a protective father to his family.
And I loved him.
It was love at first sight.
And I wanted to be with him,
to experience his love and protection.

I expressed my desire many times to my family.
But no-one listened or cared.

So I rolled under the barrier –
it was quite easy, and I did it quickly –
And I fell down into his moat.

Oh bliss! He came to me.
He whooshed me through the water – such a game! –
Then picked me up.

I faced him, looking up at him, my admired friend.
For a moment, we held hands.
He turned me round and wondered at my clothes.
And then – oh horror! –
a loud noise hit him. His grip on me loosened.
He and I fell.
And I was taken from him. – For ever! –
My love had destroyed him.

In the years that followed
I thought about this lesson
and avoided love, certainly its expression.

But every day, now no longer a child,
I go to that zoo, visit his family,
and say, Sorry, Sorry Sorry!

1 June 2016

UNCONTROLLED DESIRE

We cooked fish;
and yes, a lingering trace remained,
enticingly wafting out
to where the ginger tom,
to where the white with marmalade,
lay;
seducing them to our door;
daring them to sniff their way in,
enquiring and yes desiring.

Desire so much stronger
than shyness or any good manners,

Purring and rubbing and turning,
unable to contain their desire.

Andorra
2012?

SINCERITY

Well, if you leave the door open,
you must expect me to come in;
You have such nice, soft, carpets, chairs and beds,
so many legs where I can sharpen my claws.

And yes, I like the milk.

But I like a little cuddle too,
a human touch, a human stroke
from time to time.

And to prove it, you see, I left a few creamy laps
at the bottom of your best cracked bowl.

Ordino
August 2012

FAMILIAR[14]

You are right. I am not a cat.

I have the trappings, yes: a tail,
a marmalade coat, loud purr,
whiskers and claws.

I have the personality, too.
I am driven by curiosity,
like my independence,
and persist
when there is something I really want to have or do.
I take an interest
in things that move like a bird, a bee, a lizard, or rat.

Indeed, I also like milk and simply adore fish.

I can open doors with a tap of a curving foot,
jump high to enter a forbidden room
through a not quite closed window,
suddenly appearing in a kitchen
and startling a housewife,
who may wield her broom to banish me,
if not fly with me
through the clouds of a moonlit night.

But you know how I know where you are,
even when you are hidden,
how I appear when not quite bidden.

You have seen me sit on a low wall,
watching you prune and murder your summer lavender,
looking up at you from time to time,
and talking in a friendly way
inconsequentially but ever so companionably.

I am not a cat but your familiar.

Andorra
24 October 2015

CAT CRADLES

Sitting in the middle of the road,
looking down at them as they walk away,
I wonder, will I see them again?
They're getting old too.

I do know them well.
But scents and tastes, small noises and stirrings
distract me more and more.

When they return, I may forget
to run out to greet them,
omit to speak to them,
neglect to rub myself
around their legs.

As my ninth life nears its end,
forgetfulness begins to catch even me,
who caught so much and so many in my times.

Perhaps I should say a final Goodbye;
so that they and I can cradle close
memories of a long friendship,
and, yes, affection,
untainted by future failings,
unwilled, unwelcome, but perhaps inevitable.

Miaow….

Andorra
28 August 2017

WATCHING THE LEMURS AT THE ZOO

There were three of them.

Attracted by an awful din (maybe
provoked by teasing watchers-by),
I stood quietly to watch. Saw how
you sprung from branch to branch,
bounded to where another was two bounds ago,
sniffed at the place, then sat there;
saw how you glanced at me from time to time,
conspicuous by being inconspicuous, quiet and still.

Saw how you stood to show that you could;
reached for a twig, to show you know about tools;
saw the sudden vigorous grooming
first of underbelly and then tail;
saw how you gravitate together,
touching, lying on each other's backs,
or just sitting, hanging about near.

Saw how you carefully defecate
holding your buttocks out over a branch,
with tail carefully extended.

Saw how bird calls attract you.

It was pretty much all there, individuals' life in society,
trained to do this and that, enjoying it, showing off,
yet conscious of other ways.

BIRDS THAT AMAZE

Seven-thirty is the time for birds to amaze:

For doves to sit, supine – not "alas" – on the grass;[15]
For the crane to rise, harsh-calling, again and again,
from the rock in the man-made lake,
where crane verisimilitudes still stand;
For the seven sisters – sometimes as many as twelve –
to swoop low in a group, over the rocks,
up to lampposts and palm-trees.

But mostly still half asleep, they voice short cries,
with only an occasional – round, but tentative – trill.

A plastic bowl lies on the paving
under the water fountain.
A baseball cap lies, lost,
on the artificial grass of the playing field.
An occasional turd disturbs.
A runner walks.
Tennis-players tap a lazily bouncing ball.

We walking humans are bound to the ground;
even our dogs correctly leashed
(though some still able to sniff,
in a friendly way, our lower parts,
 and offer a lick).
The small sandy tidal beach bears
the usual assorted jetsam and flotsam.

Silent now, the crane stands looking out to sea.
A flock of egrets rises and circles.

Close by a sea-eagle swoops and veers.
A walker makes for the park-side loo.

Back at the lake,
fifteen minutes later than usual,
the tiny kingfisher sports
his bright colours of turquoise and rust,
displays his well-known, proud, watching posture.

Back at home from this morning walk,
I hear the squeaking of fairly familiar
 – even familial – birds, sitting
on my outside, wall-hanging, air-conditioner.

What a weight of things holds us down,
bound to the earth. What would it be to soar,
possession-less,
programmed by destiny
or our species' centuries-long experience,
aiming always at a specified, known, 'though distant, shore?

Discovery Bay,
Lantau, Hong Kong SAR
29 January 2017
The second day of the Year of the Fiery Rooster

SONG OF THE UPROOTED TREES

Friends, we did our best.
We stretched and spread our roots
as far as the shallow earth,
constricting concrete, and nearby
buildings would allow.

We bowed before the mighty wind,
imploring mercy ... Who would not wish
longer life?

Some of us were old – so very old –
a hundred years they said, or more
 – some, much more;
and some were very young indeed,
slender saplings – mere babes in the wood,
to coin a phrase.

Friends, what have we done to you
that you deny us growth,
sufficient rootedness
and space?

We have cleaned your air, given
you shade, whispered sweet
nothings in your ear.

We have inspired your poets,
rocked your cradles,
given graveyards dignity.

We have consented for your dogs to pee on us,
bird-fanciers to hang cages on us;
lovers to carve their names on us;
your children to climb on us,
build tree houses, swing on us.

We have given you fruit;

and as for that old story
about the apple,
was that our fault or was it yours?

The knowledge that you bought then
destroys the earth,
brings the big wind,
destroys us too.

But we, like you, we like it here;
we did prefer the green and pleasant land of Eden;
but even now there is much beauty in the natural world.
We and you share it, and are part of it.

Remember this, remember us,
make provision for all our children,
for our and your grandchildren,
so when the next big wind comes,
we may all still stand.

2018
Written in Hong Kong
after the passage of Super Typhoon Mangkhut

Grandfather's Robin   55

PARTIALITY

The Moon looks not at us
as we look at her.
Indifferent to us mortals,
she shines,
accepting the sun's light.

BLACK PLASTIC BAG

If I was a frightened cat or child,
Someone would rescue me,
climb up the tree when the weather is mild,
and release me
to live the life I was made for.

And I – I am blameless.
I didn't choose to climb up here,
propelled by adventure or curiosity.
Someone let go of me.
A gust of wind lifted me high
and the tree caught me tight,
whirled me around and impaled me.

Ever since,
when the wind enables me,
I frantically gesture for notice,[16]
but no-one cares.

I could be here forever,
a doomed immortal,
suffering the heat and the cold,
but mostly the pain of neglect.

How <u>could</u> you all leave me up here?
I was destined to help you,
to contain what you have rejected.

I beg you, release me
from my tree-top purgatory,
to do what I was made for!

Hong Kong SAR
17 January 2017
Discovery Bay, Lantau

SOCIETY

BEYOND 1997

If we could have looked beyond 30 June 1997,
we would not have imagined this –
better English, friendly taxi-drivers,
high-end boutiques, conversations on trams;

Because we are now seen as visitors, and hospitality is virtuous,
Because we are getting older and respect is virtuous,
Because we taught their children and loyalty is virtuous.

Because some remember the past fondly,

and we represent the past.

Grandfather's Robin   61

ANDORRA

The only daughter of Charlemagne
lies delectably among the mountains,
Her limbs, sprawled along the valleys,
Her hair, flowing over the summits,
Her smile warming with the daily sun;
Embraced by natives,
Sought by visitors from many lands.

On Festive days she raises herself
and shows herself
in the highways and markets of the city;
regal, upright, unbending,
not to be touched.[17]

But, everywhere, in valleys and villages,
the virgin mother of God
lives and has power.
Her sympathetic tears flow as the fruitful rivers,
teaching compassion, love;
reminding of a source of life,
higher than the hills.

Andorra,
24 October 2015

GIFTS

I never get a present I don't like, do you?
But sometimes I change my mind about what I like,
for the sake of the thank-you letter.

Yet every Christmas people write to newspapers,
dissatisfied with what they were given;
and shops exchange unwelcome and wrong-size gifts.

As for deities, they receive strange gifts all the time,
as humans judge:

"Best socks" (in a fancy packet)
before a small shrine to Mother and Child
in a Romanian church of St George.

Maybe they were offered to baby Jesus,
assuming he, too, is, or will soon be, a soccer fan?

The bottle of San Miguel,
before a similarly small,
Chinese, shrine
to the fishermen's goddess of mercy,
Tin Hau,
whom I consider would prefer
delicate Chinese tea in a tiny cup
and never would down a bottleful of beer.

But I do not think the gods reject
what men have offered them; or criticise the gifts.

Maybe immortals see
that the giver gave
the most cherished thing they owned;
and value the sacrifice.

Better to worship gods with gifts
Than stretch our minds
to gift those who will despise them.

24 October 2015

FORTUNE'S WHEEL

Technology works.

Men get put on the moon.
A number dialled in Hong Kong
wakes friends in New York

But psychology, sociology,
politics, economics,
do <u>they</u> work?

The text-books which explain these studies
are impressive, fascinating.

But what useful applications have they had?

What success have <u>they</u> had
in perfecting the lot of man?

Look around, and see!

Twenty percent of adults
suffer some mental illness.

Diplomacy constantly fails.

The world's economies spin
in uncontrollable spirals,
crazy bar-charts,
upwards and downwards,
dizzying both rich or poor.

The sixteenth century and earlier
viewed Fortune as a woman
and imagined all of us
sitting on her wheel.

– "Turn thy wheel once more!"
the blinded Duke of Gloucester said
in Shakespeare's play, *King Lear,*
hoping, "this too will pass." –

Do we, 21st century people,
also accept this?
Or do we want more?

c. 1982; edited 2006; revised 2007

MACHINES ARE NOT YET HUMAN

Machines can do a lot of things
but can they go to the toilet?
Do they know to put their hand in another's
and walk firmly to the back of the ferry, say,
when it's not alongside,
or down the corridor of the train,
when it's not standing at the station?
Or do they just plop oil,
anywhere and any when they like?

– Some *people* of course also can't read!

Hong Kong
1 June 2016

BETTER?

Better to have loved and lost
Than never to have loved at all.

But is it better
To have put a plant on your balcony
and then let it die unbecomingly?

Better to have gone for the climb and broken a leg
Than never to have set foot on the mountain?

Better to have taken the bend at high speed and crashed
Than to have remained frustrated behind the unarticulated lorry?

Better to have jumped overboard to save a child and drown
Than to watch the child itself drown in your sight?

What is better, really?

15 December 2016

SONG OF THE POTATO[18]

The potato family – of which I am one –
is large, living in many lands.
Growing in the dark,
we show ourselves in light.

Like the emblemed pelican,
feeding its young with blood
from its own breast,
we feed the human family
from that which gives us growth,
sacrificing,
that even the poor may live.

Use us well, human families!
Choose among us,
in each place where you live,
those who are hardy.

Take a lesson
from Ireland,
from their past Potato Famine.

Follow Bolivia!
Respect the food security we give!
Enjoy the peace
that full bellies provide!

2019

EKPHRASIS

Responses and thoughts about exhibitions

VISIONS ON SHOW

"Ten² Inches Sculpture Exhibition"[19]

The roots of childhood dreams hang in the air,
reaching a long way down for the nourishment of reality,
but the ladder leading to the house in the trees stands on air, too.
If we want to reach it, we need the purchase of hope.

The bronze cow – "Energetic" – has no moon to jump over;
The bronze teddy bear is not really hugging a thorn;
But the wooden sculpture called "the body"
demonstrates the balance of practised strength
pierced by a carved encircled Pisces to liven things up.

Hong Kong
October 2018
Hong Kong Festival Fringe

OUTCASTS FROM REALITY (*short version*)

*Dialogue at the opening of the Wattis Fine Art exhibition,
"Hong Kong Early Photography c. 1868-1925".*

"And who are they?"
the visitor from Central Europe asked,
nodding at the other gallery guests,
as we mildly sipped a glass of wine,
viewing the work of Afong,
R. C. Hurley, and yes, Anon.

"Collectors, I suppose?" "Yes.
Collectors,
publishers, historians
of nineteenth-century
Hong Kong."

"Ah," she says, not missing a beat;
"Other outcasts from reality!"

"Outcasts"? – Refugees, perhaps....

Are these the names for those
who study, who even may
appreciate, past worlds?

We have other lives outside,
in the busy streets and offices
of Asia's World City.

That city's past partly
explains our presence here,
certainly clarifies,
gives roots to our present lives,
burnishes the services
we are called to offer now.

We help the past communicate;
help it link with the present future,
which in turn fulfills, extends the past.

Not outcasts then, nor refugees. –

Transmitters in time and space,
of what our enquiring minds seek out;
communicators to "the general"[20]
of what we, after some study, understand.

30 June 2011

OUTCASTS FROM REALITY[21] (*longer version*)

"And who are they?"
the visitor from Central Europe asked,
nodding at the other gallery guests,
as we mildly sipped a glass of wine,
viewing the work of Afong,
R. C. Hurley, and yes, Anon.

"Collectors, I suppose?" "Yes. Collectors,
publishers, historians of nineteenth-
century Hong Kong", I replied.

"Ah," she says, without missing a beat;
"Other outcasts from reality!"

She is thinking of her mother, it seems,
who, she felt, refused
to live in socialist reality
in Czechoslovak lands,
post 1948, when Russia had dominance.

She encouraged her daughter,
born the same year,
to think what they taught at school
was "nonsense".

And the girl's private reading too
came from the past –
The Swiss Family Robinson, Kipling's
The Jungle Story, Shakespeare, Conrad,
Goethe, Molière, Dostoevsky –
the varied classics of our European
culture.

She is thinking also of herself, I think,
translating and dubbing others' words and works
for thirty-five years;
isolated with them
in the dark of a recording studio
– a cellar as she has called it –
consciously self-exiled
from outside society;
her thoughts, though, winging free.

But "outcasts"? – Refugees, perhaps....

And we in the exhibition
opening, in a Hong Kong gallery;
are we outcasts, or even refugees,
as we study, appreciate the world as it was?

We have other lives outside,
in the busy streets and offices
of Asia's World City;
which the city's past partly explains,
certainly clarifies,
gives roots to our present lives;
and burnishes the services
we are called to offer now.

We help the past communicate;
help it link with the present, future,
which fulfill, connect, and extend the past.

Not outcasts then, nor refugees. –

Transmitters in time and space,
of what we view with our enquiring minds;
speaking out our understandings
to "the general"!

30 June 2011

Grandfather's Robin   77

SCENES and MOODS

SCENE BY THE CHINA SEA

The sharp smell of bleeding vegetation,
cut in the morning of this perfect day,
mingles
with the familiar resinous tang
of leaking pines

as children run
and adults open themselves
under the sun
on this scantily populated
beach by the China Sea.

Discovery Bay,
Hong Kong SAR
2012

SADNESS

Eating alone
when Christmas muzak is playing
is sadness;

Rows of potted Christmas poinsettias,
dressed in gold paper,
lined up
in uncaring long walkways
are sadness;

a red light flashing on and off,
automatically,
is sadness.

So are the rows of red lanterns, in bleak parking lots,
however thoughtfully hung there,
at Chinese New Year.

16 October 2012; 31 January 2017

ACHING FOR TREES

I ache for trees massed on the hills,
Mixing their various leaves,
Talking, climbing the slope,
Conversing with the breeze.

Once I could have known their lives,
Their familiar insects, birds and other small creatures,
The winds that moved them and the sun that warmed.

But that is the past.

Now I crave the masses of people,
Their gales of laughter,
Air that is machinery-cooled,
Flowers in a vase or manicured garden,
Alas.

Andorra,
Summer 2016

THREE BELLS IN A PYRENEAN VILLAGE[22]

The old church tower stands patiently,
Making no comment,
The warm lunar light revealing faithfully
The mechanism, pulleys and ropes of the old cracked bell,
Used to penetrate and punctuate the day, calling to worship.

A small alien bell in the small village square
rings the quiet beginning of meditation,
Not hugely different in intention, perhaps,
from the communion bell, rung out more loudly,
inside the church, here, daily, for centuries.

The still presence of the solid stone church
Backgrounds the lower, smaller, changing lights
of the not-quite-yet hypnotic,
ever-changing, psychedelic, slide-show,
aiming to support the efforts
 – honest efforts –
of three visiting artistes.

Gradually the drums, guitar and keyboard
Take on a rhythm that the organ and choir
Have never sounded.

Small dogs trot past, taking an informed
Interest in the people sitting, chilly, at outside tables,
Slightly attentive to the one-night summer-holiday show.

Small children run about the tables,
Which hold drinks, mountain salads and today's fresh bread.

Communion with a known god
is a ritual, familiar
even to those who are absent (most of those here)
when the village priest calls God's people
to gather at His always welcoming table.

This bell, this rhythm, this novelty
lack drawing power; fail to reach the spiritual,
in a crowd, expecting an entertaining evening,
with perhaps some lively rhythm to dance to.

Ordino,
Principat d'Andorra
21 August 2019

EARLY MORNING

No kingfisher, no crow.
But I know that a bird is there from that darkness on a tree.

A bird shows its presence by a darkness on a tree.

Are we darkness on the earth? – Showing our presence

      by the negatives we cause?

Electric light a blossom.

Baseball cap hung on the water fountain.
A child's vest too.
Dead – by whose hand?

Discovery Bay,
Hong Kong SAR
2018

SURVIVAL

MIRRORED

I look at my hands and see
my mother's hands in older age.

Passing a mirror, I see her glance out at me.

And from my lips emerge, from time to time,
selections from my father's strict views.

The former please me, the latter amuse.

When I die,
I will carry their echoes, their influence no more;
they will die too;
unless a pupil or friend caught some glimmers too,
passing them on and on.

I do hope so.

28 August 2017

A NEW NOAH'S ARK?

We learnt the lesson long ago,
made a pact, "Adapt to survive":
We grew wings, shed fins,
changed colour, found new habitats.
But now, external changes move too fast
for our leisurely process
of multi-generational response.

We are dwindling, dying out, disappearing.

This world's Noah's Ark is carrying us
 to destruction not salvation.

There is no place from which a dove
can bring us the green leaf of hope
as evidence it exists.

One of our species, man,
has better learnt than we
to adapt – not himself – but the environment
for his own... survival...

well, for the pleasure and profit, now,
of those, born in places where
successive scientific revolutions
have made survival
less of a full-time task
than it is for us; and which,
at one time,
it also was for them.

Some of them, now, fear
that matters have gone too far,
that they have secured for the world
 an uninhabitable future.

They talk of space-flight
and colonies on other planets
as the survival option.

But will they take us with them?
Are they building now
a noah's ark
for species other than their own?

And if they could and do...
in a few eons time,
would we not arrive again
at the same place?

Flight may indeed be a solution
for a while. Many of us
know the need to leave and return,
leave and return,
as the seasons change and change.

But is there no choice but this?
We like it here. We know it here.
We know the behaviours to employ.

That species – man – is clever
in ways we have not learnt.

Can we teach them to apply their minds
to learn some of our own intelligences?
– to kill only to eat; to adapt;
not force creation as a whole to adapt to them?

Is it so difficult to enjoy what now exists?
To refrain from changing – and thus destroying – all?

COMFORT[23]

Do the stars write us,
rescue us from oblivion,
even death?

Is it a conscious, loving act,
as Paz presents it?

Are they determined
that no human should be trashed?

I wonder.

However close they look sometimes,
the stars are a long way off,
as Malfi's Duchess said.[24]

Would not details become blurred,
facts forgotten or confused on the way;
and the writing-down
resemble us, only in part, if at all?

Moreover, can the stars really feel
benign, have purposes,
and the power to accomplish them?

As for God's recording angel,
writing down pluses and minuses
of word, thought, and deed,
how wholly true is the record which he makes?

His bureaucratic task surely needs
the help of many clerks. They may lose
attention, go out for a smoke or a pee,
be checking their messages,
when a particularly good or bad
event occurs.

The notes, <u>possibly</u> made by the stars,
and — metaphorically at least —
<u>certainly</u> made by the angel in charge of records,
are surely incomplete, if not untrue;
cannot represent each of us in whole.

And indeed, as Paz himself
notes elsewhere,
words are deficient in conveying
what we (and surely therefore they)
entirely mean.

***

What other comfort can be found?

Our souls, as Marvell says, may rise like birds
and preen their feathers
in God's eternal sun;[25]

our bodies
— grown from the general matter
from which existences take form —
mix with earth and air and sea;
and are — in eternity's good time — re-used,
following Nature's rules.

It might be good for us
to focus
on the elements
of the created, evolved world;
what we might have been,
and could become.

May be saving from extinction
a plant, a butterfly, a bird
saves our own reincarnated, metamorphosed,
transmogrified future forms;
rescues the forms of those who have lived before.

***

As John Donne has said,[26]
send not to ask for whom the tolling bell
resounds.
Its lamentation is for us.

All is flux says Heraclitus.[27] And we
are part of all.

August 2015

A SINGLE DAHLIA

A single dahlia on a very small patch of cared-for lawn,
solitary, brave,
signaling – no, not a place of burial –
but beauty and peace achieved, an offer of joy,

witness of the possible,
a hope for something larger,
a wider expanse of confirmed,
carefully-tended,
peace and happiness for all.

Andorra
28 August 2017

SHORT POEMS

TRUE RECORD[28]

Here I stand
writing poems on the stones in the park;
swiftly drawing; guards ignoring;
using water. Poems fade
and disappear. In my heart
are always clear.

9 March 2016

NO NEED TO HURRY![29]

Here I am, carrying flowers
for the funeral, and the signs
to tell you where to go.
No need to hurry.
Death will catch you too.

9 March 2016

CONSTANT PARADE[30]

Wearing my best hat and ear-rings,
I sit in the glow of the life
I have lived;
thinking of him – the husband I had
or the one I didn't – hardly seeing
the constant parade and flow of life
that passes and re-passes me
as I think of the past and ponder
my future.

9 March 2016

CHRISTMAS HAIKU 2012
(5/7/5)

In the snow sun sand
Turkeys wish they could be stuffed
And cranberries crammed.

Hong Kong
20 December 2012
Writers' Circle Christmas Party

CHRISTMAS HAIKU 2013
(5/7/5)

Silently falling
snow stars shepherds heralding
amazing future

Hong Kong
10 December 2013
Writers' Circle Christmas Party

IT HAPPENS

An older, tall woman searched my face.
I smiled.
She saw my smile and she smiled too.

TWIN EGGS

Two eggs in a cracked bowl.
Not quite the same shape,
but perfectly joined.

31 January 2017

RIDDLE

Pink on ears
Pink on tail
But shouldn't it rather be
pink in knees?

What am I?

GIRLS GET THEIR MAN

"Wedding here is a soul dream – realise it!"

The proud hotel poster shows
three rows of pearls
circling the entrance path,
looking like pearly whites,
innocent-looking as a shark's jaw.

GOTCHA!

Hong Kong,
1 October 2011

THE PRICE OF BEAUTY

A golden tree – mimosa –
Half-broken by its blossoms

Golden girls – oh, so
Burdened with your bling!

27 April 2013

RETIRING[31]

The ending is the beginning
enriched by previous endings
and all the time between them,
as we may <u>try</u> to know.

2003, Revised 2006

ADVANCE COMMENT

So many reasons to enjoy Gillian Bickley's luminous poetry –
humor, depth and wisdom. Through her verse we feel deep
empathy for a grandfather, a bus driver, a waiter offering soft food
to toothless aunties and grandmas, a beloved housekeeper.
It is a measure of Gillian Bickley's humanity, that she feels the
wonder and dilemma of our shared lives with each other, with cats,
birds, lemurs, and a gorilla. She speaks for the trees. Bickley takes
us to her Pyrenees, to Andorra – exotic and mundane.
Lovely and evocative, Bickley's powers of observation and precise,
selective description lend many of these poems the power of fine
portraiture, a sepia photograph, where we see into the eyes, where
we discover essence.

Jack Mayer
Vermont
25 June 2020

ADVANCE COMMENT

In this work, Gillian Bickley affords us a glimpse into her
perspective. She invites us to reflect on the rich tapestry of life and
our shared human experience. Why should you read this collection?
Because there is no greater privilege than intimacy.

Mary-Jane Newton
Oxford
UK
17 July 2020

ADVANCE COMMENT

Grandfather's Robin, as Gillian Bickley notes in her brief introduction, is a *recollection*, drawing together fragments of experience since her last collection in 2012 but also from the whole of her life. Poetry "takes its origin," as Wordsworth wrote, "from emotion recollected in tranquility." What begins with a "spontaneous overflow of powerful feelings" ends in carefully chosen words that bring to mind what "caused them to be written down." In 'Soft' (24), describing a 2013 encounter with a young waiter in Hong Kong, she writes, "Sometimes, when we speak, our lives unroll / Before those we speak to, without our knowing." That image of our lives unrolling in our words without our knowing captures the spirit of this collection perfectly – poems as moments of tranquility in which we can encounter lives unrolling in times that (as 'Beyond 1997' subtly reminds us) are anything but. To make a record such as this is a good resolution indeed, and I am pleased that Gillian has chosen for the cover a moment of tranquility I painted. As Mrs. Dorothy Collins might have said (32), reflecting, as these poems do, the quietness of a life-long practice, "Very well!"

Steven Schroeder
Chicago
15 June 2020

[1] After reading the poem, 'Hear the rain', by Octavio Paz.

[2] Patchwork artist, Valerie Rymarenko, told the writer that when she is working on a patchwork, it tells her when it is finished and also what its name is.

[3] From Gerard Manley-Hopkins, "This Jack, joke, poor potsherd, patch, matchwood, immortal diamond, / Is immortal diamond." ('That Nature Is a Heraclitean Fire and of the Comfort of the Resurrection', last two lines.)

[4] Geoffrey Bonsall was deputy librarian at the University of Hong Kong, then director of the University's Press; later, under the name, Charles Weatherall, he was a broadcaster for RTHK. He was a skilled interpreter of the shorthand used by the artist, George Chinnery (1774-1852).

[5] The narrator speaks only a few words of Cantonese; and only the young man speaks English.
In an earlier poem, 'Language Lessons' (*Moving House and other Poems from Hong Kong*, 2005), I have described a similar experience, when another accompanying husband has taken a degree of responsibility for my welfare in a hospital queue, also in a way entirely natural to him.

[6] A nine-year-old boy, living on the Mainland of China, went missing in 1996. His distraught mother searched the country, looking for him, without success. Twenty-two years later, after an illness of about ten years, she died from breast cancer, having previously asked her sister to ensure her corneas were given, so she could "see" her son if he ever came home. Her corneas have now been given to two young patients with eye diseases.

This poem is written in two parts. The first part is in the voice of the mother and the second part in the voice of the two young patients who received her corneas.

The boy apparently had a scar on his heel.

The following is the full text of the SCMP article.
"SICHUAN–A mother offered her corneas for transplant in the hope of 'gazing' on her son from beyond the grave more than two decades after he went missing, a local newspaper reports.

Wang Shiqun, from Yibin, died last week aged 55 after battling breast cancer for almost a decade. She asked her younger sister to ensure her corneas were given to a donor [*sic*] so she could once more 'see' her son if he ever came home, *Chengdu Economic Daily* reported on Thursday.

Her son Zhu Hai was aged nine and living with his father after the couple's divorce when he went missing after school on June 4,1996. Hai's cousin was reported to have told their grandmother the boy had said at a school gathering three days earlier: 'Let us toast to this final occasion we will be together.'

Wang had travelled across the country to Kunming, Beijing, Chengdu and other cities in search of her son, who has a scar on his heel, and had been given several false leads by people.

In 2010, Wang was diagnosed with breast cancer, and before an operation in October she mentioned donating her corneas. 'When she left, she simply refused to close her eyes,' her sister said. 'I told her I would definitely help her find her son.'

Wang's corneas have been given to two young patients with eye diseases."

[7] In the long short story, 'The Portrait of Dorian Grey' by Oscar Wilde, a handsome young man remains youthful in appearance until his death, whereas a portrait of him ages in his place.

[8] Mrs Collins was a senior lecturer in Chemistry at the University of Hong Kong for a large number of years and passed away at the China Coast Community in Kowloon Tong, Hong Kong. "Very well" is the response she often gave, when asked to do something or other. While obviously signalling that she would do what was asked, it was never clear to the writer whether she was really happy with the requests to which she assented.

[9] After seeing the 2016-2017 Keats-Shelley Prize call for entries on the theme, 'To a Friend', to celebrate the 200th anniversary of the publication of Keats' first poetry collection.

[10] If you would like to know more about the life, death, and influence

of Saint Maximilian Maria Kolbe, you can find a great deal of information on the internet.

[11] Samuel Isaac Joseph Schereschewsky, Bishop of the American Episcopal Mission appointed to China, translated the Book of Common Prayer into Chinese as well as the Christian Bible. He worked to the end of his life, reduced to typing with one finger for the last eight years and confined to a wheel-chair. A speaker at the Conference, "Learning form the Past, Looking to the Future: Anglican-Episcopal History in China and its Impact on the Church Today" (held 7-9 June 2012 at the Hong Kong Mariners' Club, Organised by the HKSKH Standing Commission of Theological Education and SKH Ming Hua Theological College), questioned whether this was a suitable use of Schereschewsky's life, given, partly, that his method is now regarded as in error.

[12] Written in response to the earlier edited video showing Harambe the western lowland silverback gorilla evidently protecting the small child that had fallen into the gorilla enclosure at Cincinatti Zoo, and also bearing in mind the comment that the child had several times expressed a desire to go into the enclosure. The zoo authorities killed Harambe, to protect the child. The rest is imagination based on this information and focusing, not on what was the right or wrong thing to do, or on blaming anyone, but imagining what impact this event will have had on the child, when a grown man.

[13] Revised after viewing unedited video and originally-seen video again, online.

[14] Title and last word suggested by Verner Bickley

[15] A reference to American Gertrude Stein's poem, which includes this statement.

[16] Maya Miteva of Bulgaria inspired this poem. I uploaded a short video of a black plastic bag trapped on the top of a tree and asked, "A little quirky, perhaps. But see what you think now lives in the tree outside my window!" What I remembered, at the time of writing this, was that Maya replied, "It is a poem frantically gesturing to get you to notice it." But when I checked what she had actually said, I found the following automatic translation, "I think in Tree lives a parasitic poem

furiously is begging to be noticed by you." Perhaps I should write another poem in which I focus more on the idea of a "parasitic" poem.

[17] The "Giants" (huge model figures) paraded in Andorra La Vella, capital city of the Co-Principality of Andorra, include a representation of Charlemagne's daughter. It is to Charlemagne that the people of Andorra attribute their independence. The virgin Mary, as Our Lady of Meritxell, is the patron saint of the Co-Principality.

[18] This portrayal of the pelican occurs in western Europe as early as the Renaissance.
As for the potato, one of the points made about the Potato Famine in Ireland is that only one variety of potato was cultivated. (See https://en.wikipedia.org/wiki/Monoculture.)
When writing this poem, by invitation, I also read that the particular type of potato was unsuitable for the environment.

[19] This exhibition was organized by "Hong Kong Sculpture", at the Hong Kong Festival Fringe Club, Fringe, 12–23 October 2018.

[20] An allusion to the saying, "It's caviar to the general", used by Hamlet in Shakespeare's play of that name.

[21] Following the opening of the Wattis Fine Art exhibition, "Hong Kong Early Photography c. 1868-1925", attended with Czech author, Olga Walló, soon after publication in English translation of "Tightrope! – A Bohemian Tale", the middle novel of Walló's autobiographical trilogy.

[22] Written in the Main Square, Ordino, Principat d'Andorra during the concert, "Música ètnica pel despertar de la consciència." – "Ethnic Music for the awakening of consciousness" given by Concert Amaru, as part of the – Cicle Nits Obertes – Open Nights Series, organised by the Tourist Office of the Ordino Comu (parish).

[23] After reading the poems, 'Brotherhood' and 'The word outloud' by Octavio Paz.

[24] In John Webster's play, *The Duchess of Malfi,* after the eponymous heroine has cursed the stars, the villain, Bosola taunts her, "Look you,

the stars shine still." She retorts, "My curse hath a great way to go".

25 An allusion to the poem, 'The Garden' by English poet and civil servant, Andrew Marvell (1621-1678):
"My soul into the boughs does glide;
There like a bird it sits and sings,
Then whets, and combs its silver wings;
And, till prepar'd for longer flight,
Waves in its plumes the various light." (verse 7, ll. 4-8)

26 John Donne (1572-1631): English poet and clergyman of the Church of England. His sermon, *Devotions Upon Emergent Occasions* XVII (1623), contains the much quoted words: "No man is an island, entire of itself; every man is a piece of the Continent, a part of the main.... Any man's death diminishes me, for I am involved in mankind. Any therefore never send to know for whom the bell tolls; it tolls for thee".

27 Saying attributed to Greek philosopher, Heraclitus (544BC-483BC).

28 Responding to a photo of a Chinese man, writing poems in water.

29 Responding to a photo of a young man, walking the middle of a road, carrying a funeral wreath.

30 Responding to a photo of an old lady, sitting at a street café.

31 Written in response to a request for each colleague to contribute a poem on the occasion of the retirement of one member of the Department.

SOME POETRY AND POETRY COLLECTIONS
Published by Proverse Hong Kong

IN ENGLISH

A Gateway Has Opened, by Liam Blackford. 2021.

Alphabet, by Andrew S. Guthrie. 2015.

Astra and Sebastian, by L.W. Illsley. 2011.

Black Holes Within Us (translation from Macedonian),
by Marta Markoska. 2021

Bliss of Bewilderment, by Birgit Bunzel Linder. 2017.

The Burning Lake, by Jonathan Locke Hart. 2016.

Celestial Promise, by Hayley Ann Solomon. 2017.

Chasing light, by Patricia Glinton Meicholas. 2013.

China suite and other poems, by Gillian Bickley. 2009.

Entanglements: Physics, love, and wilderness dreams,
by Jack Mayer, 2022.

Epochal Reckonings, by J.P. Linstroth. 2020.

For the record and other poems of Hong Kong,
by Gillian Bickley. 2003.

Frida Kahlo's cry and other poems,
by Laura Solomon. 2015.

Grandfather's Robin, by Gillian Bickley. 2020.

Heart to Heart: Poems, by Patty Ho. 2010.

H/ERO/T/IC BOOK (translation from Macedonian),
by Marta Markoska. 2020.

Home, away, elsewhere, by Vaughan Rapatahana. 2011.

Hong Kong Growing Pains, by Jon Ng. 2020.

Immortelle and bhandaaraa poems,
by Lelawattee Manoo-Rahming. 2011.

In vitro, by Laura Solomon. 2nd ed. 2014.

Irreverent poems for pretentious people,
by Henrik Hoeg. 2016.

The layers between (essays and poems),
by Celia Claase. 2015.

Of leaves & ashes, by Patty Ho. 2016.

Life Lines, by Shahilla Shariff. 2011.

Moving house and other poems from Hong Kong,
by Gillian Bickley. 2005.

Over the Years: Selected Collected Poems, 1972-2015,
by Gillian Bickley. 2017.

Painting the borrowed house: poems, by Kate Rogers. 2008.

Perceptions, by Gillian Bickley. 2012.

Please Stand Back from the Platform Door,
by Vishal Nanda. 2021.

Poems from the Wilderness, by Jack Mayer. 2020.

Rain on the pacific coast, by Elbert Siu Ping Lee. 2013.

refrain, by Jason S. Polley. 2010.

Savage Charm, by Ahmed Elbeshlawy. 2019.

Seeking Solace, by Nikhil Parekh, 2022.

Shadow play, by James Norcliffe. 2012.

Shadows in deferment, by Birgit Bunzel Linder. 2013.

Shifting sands, by Deepa Vanjani. 2016.

Sightings: a collection of poetry, with an essay, 'Communicating Poems',
by Gillian Bickley. 2007.

Smoked pearl: poems of Hong Kong and beyond,
by Akin Jeje (Akinsola Olufemi Jeje). 2010.

Of symbols misused, by Mary-Jane Newton. 2011.

The Hummingbird Sometimes Flies Backwards,
by D.J. Hamilton. 2019.

The Year of the Apparitions,
by José Manuel Sevilla. 2020.

Uncharted Waters, by Paola Caronni, 2021.

Unlocking, by Mary-Jane Newton. March 2014.

Violet, by Carolina Ilica. March 2019.

Wonder, lust & itchy feet, by Sally Dellow. 2011.

POETRY ANTHOLOGIES
Published by Proverse Hong Kong

Mingled voices: the international Proverse Poetry Prize anthology 2016, edited by Gillian and Verner Bickley. 2017.

Mingled voices 2: the international Proverse Poetry Prize anthology 2017, edited by Gillian and Verner Bickley. 2018.

Mingled voices 3: the international Proverse Poetry Prize anthology 2018, edited by Gillian and Verner Bickley. 2019.

Mingled voices 4: the international Proverse Poetry Prize anthology 2019, edited by Gillian and Verner Bickley. 2020.

Mingled voices 5: the international Proverse Poetry Prize anthology 2020, edited by Gillian and Verner Bickley. 2021.

Mingled voices 6: the international Proverse Poetry Prize anthology 2021, edited by Gillian and Verner Bickley. 2022.

Mingled voices 7: the international Proverse Poetry Prize anthology 2022, edited by Gillian and Verner Bickley. 2023. (Scheduled.)

POETRY IN CHINESE

Moving House and Other Poems, by Gillian Bickley (with additional contents & b/w photographs). Translated by Tony Yip, Joan Cho, Queenie Kung, Aster Lee, Yuk-Hang Ng, Connie Pang. Edited by Yip Ming Tak, Tony. 2008.

For the Record, by Gillian Bickley. Translated by Simon Chau. 2010, 2021.

EDUCATIONAL
(English Language)

Poems to Enjoy, Book 1, by Verner Bickley (3rd Ed) w. 1 audio CD (Graded poetry anthology w. teaching and learning notes, glossary, etc.)

Poems to Enjoy, Book 2, by Verner Bickley (3rd Ed) w. 2 audio CDs (Graded poetry anthology w. teaching and learning notes, glossary, etc.)

Poems to Enjoy, Book 3, by Verner Bickley (3rd Ed) w. 2 audio CDs (Graded poetry anthology w. teaching and learning notes, glossary, etc.)

Poems to Enjoy, Book 4, by Verner Bickley (3rd Ed) w. 2 audio CDs (Graded poetry anthology w. teaching and learning notes, glossary, etc.)

Poems to Enjoy, Book 5, by Verner Bickley (3rd Ed) w. 3 audio CDs (Graded poetry anthology w. teaching and learning notes, glossary, etc.)

FIND OUT MORE ABOUT PROVERSE AUTHORS, BOOKS, LITERARY PRIZES AND EVENTS

Visit our website: http://www.proversepublishing.com
Follow us on Twitter: twitter.com/Proversebooks
"Like" us on www.facebook.com/ProversePress
Subscribe to our youtube channel:
youtube.com/@ProversePublishing

Request our free E-Newsletter
Send your request to info@proversepublishing.com.

Availability
Available in Hong Kong and world-wide from our
Hong Kong based distributor,
The Chinese University of Hong Kong Press,
See the Proverse page on the website
https://cup.cuhk.edu.hk/Proversehk

Most titles can be ordered online from amazon
(various countries) and other online retailers.
Stock-holding retailers
Hong Kong (CUHKP, Bookazine)
Canada (Elizabeth Campbell Books),
Andorra (Llibreria La Puça, La Llibreria)
United Kingdom (Ivybridge Bookshop, Devon).
Orders may be made from bookshops
in the UK and elsewhere.
All titles may be available from Proverse Hong Kong,
http://www.proversepublishing.com

Ebooks
Most of our titles are available also as Ebooks.

Audiobooks
Some of our titles are available as audiobooks.

www.ingramcontent.com/pod-product-compliance
Lightning Source LLC
Chambersburg PA
CBHW051428150726
48000CB00005B/2007